A KID'S LIFE DURING

THE MIDDLE AGES

SARAH MACHAJEWSKI

PowerKiDS
press.

New York

Published in 2015 by The Rosen Publishing Group, Inc.
29 East 21st Street, New York, NY 10010

First Edition

Editor: Sarah Machajewski
Book Design: Michael J. Flynn

Photo Credits: Cover (artwork) LTL/Universal Images Group/Getty Images; cover, pp. 1, 3–10, 12–16, 18–20, 22–24 (background texture) Ozerina Anna/Shutterstock.com; pp. 3–10, 12–16, 18–20, 22–24 (paper) Paladin12/Shutterstock.com; p. 5 Slava Gerj/Shutterstock.com; p. 7 English School/The Bridgeman Art Library/Getty Images; p. 9 LockStockBob/Shutterstock.com; p. 11 Simon Bening/The Bridgeman Art Library/Getty Images; p. 13 Melanie Vollmert/Shutterstock.com; p. 14 McCarthy's PhotoWorks/Shutterstock.com; p. 15 Leemage/Universal Images Group/Getty Images; p. 17 De Agostini/A. Dagil Orti/De Agostini Picture Library/Getty Images; p. 18 De Agostini/A. De Gregorio/De Agostini Picture Library/Getty Images; p. 19 Heritage Images/Hulton Fine Art Collection/Getty Images; p. 21 Josse Lieferinxe/The Bridgeman Art Library/Getty Images; p. 22 Mikadun/Shutterstock.com.

Library of Congress Cataloging-in-Publication Data

Machajewski, Sarah.
  A kid's life during the Middle Ages / Sarah Machajewski.
      pages cm. — (How kids lived)
  Includes index.
  ISBN 978-1-4994-0026-7 (pbk.)
  ISBN 978-1-4994-0009-0 (6 pack)
  ISBN 978-1-4994-0019-9 (library binding)
  1. Children—Europe—History—To 1500—Juvenile literature. 2. Children—Europe—History—16th century—Juvenile literature. 3. Youth—Europe—History—To 1500—Juvenile literature. 4. Youth—Europe—History—16th century—Juvenile literature. 5. Europe—Social life and customs—To 1492—Juvenile literature. 6. Europe—Social life and customs—16th century—Juvenile literature. 7. Social history—Medieval, 500-1500—Juvenile literature. I. Title.
  HQ792.E8M325 2015
  305.2309409'031—dc23
                    2014035481

Manufactured in the United States of America

CPSIA Compliance Information: Batch #CW15PK: For Further Information contact Rosen Publishing, New York, New York at 1-800-237-9932

CONTENTS

IN BETWEEN ERAS

"Middle Ages" is the name for a period of time in European history that lasted from AD 378 to about AD 1450. Where does this name come from? This **era** was in between ancient times and modern times.

Many people believe few important things happened during the Middle Ages. However, this isn't true. Powerful rulers and great thinkers shaped life. Masterpieces were created in art, building, music, and writing. Studying the lives of ordinary people can teach us a lot about this era's **culture**.

The Middle Ages fall between the end of ancient times and the beginning of modern times.

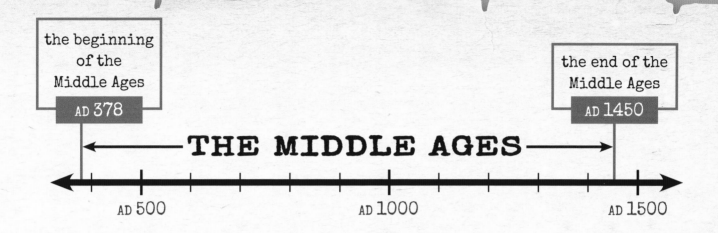

the beginning
of the
Middle Ages

AD 378

THE MIDDLE AGES

the end of the
Middle Ages

AD 1450

AD 500

AD 1000

AD 1500

MIDDLE AGES SOCIETY

In ancient times, Europe was ruled by one central government, the Western Roman Empire. This changed as Europe moved into the Middle Ages. A society of different classes developed. Kings and queens were at the top of the social ladder. Under them was a class of nobles, called lords. These two classes owned land. Most people in Middle Ages society were peasants. They were the lowest class.

The royal and noble classes held a lot of power, but there was one **institution** they answered to: the Catholic Church. The Church was the most powerful force in the Middle Ages.

This image shows one artist's idea of what a town during the Middle Ages may have been like.

MORE ROLES IN SOCIETY

Society during the Middle Ages also included knights. They were soldiers in a king or lord's army.

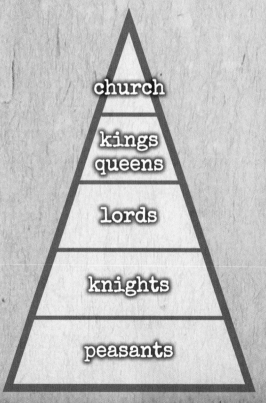

church

kings
queens

lords

knights

peasants

PEASANT VILLAGES

Isolda was a peasant girl. Like other peasant families, Isolda's family lived in a village. The village was located on land that belonged to a rich lord. The peasants in the village worked for him.

Peasant homes were very simple. Isolda's home was made of sticks, straw, and mud. The roof was made of straw and hay. There was one main room with a **hearth**. Isolda and her family slept in another room, which was very small.

The main road in Isolda's village led to the lord's castle and to the local church. These buildings were very big and beautiful.

All Isolda knew of life was what happened in her village. Few people in the Middle Ages ever traveled far from home.

PEASANT CHILDREN

Peasant children didn't have much to look forward to in life. If you were born a peasant, you would be one as an adult.

SERFDOM

A peasant's day began when the sun came up. Isolda and her family were farmers. They woke up early to begin work in the fields. Isolda's family grew wheat, beans, onions, garlic, and other vegetables.

Peasant farmers were called serfs. Serfs belonged to the lord. They gave him most of the food they grew as payment for living on his land. They also paid taxes. Some peasant farmers were free. Peasants who didn't farm may have been shopkeepers. Others practiced a trade, such as blacksmithing.

BOUND FOR LIFE

Serfs could buy their freedom, but this wasn't common. There were few ways for them to make money. Often, they were bound to the land and their lord for life.

Every person in a peasant family was needed to help work the fields, including children. They were put to work as soon as they were old enough to help.

THE PEASANT DIET

Isolda's family kept some of the food they grew. Her mom used rye to make dark bread that Isolda ate with every meal. One meal Isolda ate regularly was pottage, which was a thick stew made of grain and vegetables. Pottage cooked over a fire until the grains and vegetables were cooked all the way through.

No two pots of pottage were the same. The stew was kept over several days, and peasants added whatever food they had as the days passed. Sometimes Isolda's mom added meat if they were lucky enough to have it.

THE RICH MAN'S DIET

Isolda's lord ate far better than his peasants. He ate white bread, fish, sliced meats, cheese, fruits, and vegetables. These foods were expensive in the Middle Ages!

Isolda was in charge of tending to the pottage. She learned how to make it when she was young. This helped her mom out a lot.

DRESSING THE PART

Clothing worn in the Middle Ages depended on someone's class. Peasants like Isolda wore a tunic, which was a long shirt that ended at the knee. Isolda wore tights or socks when it was cold. Her mother wore a tunic with a kirtle over it. A kirtle was a kind of loose dress. Isolda's dad wore a tunic with wool pants underneath. Women and girls didn't wear pants.

WIMPLE

WEARING A WIMPLE

Isolda's mom covered her hair with a wimple, which she also wrapped around her neck. Isolda would have to wear this after she got married.

Rich men and women wore more expensive clothing. Rich women wore brightly colored dresses, **elaborate** hats, and **jewelry**. Rich men, like Isolda's lord, wore jackets over their tunic and tights under it.

Isolda helped her mom make clothing for her family. They made clothes out of wool and linen, a type of cloth.

A LIFE OF WORK

As a peasant born into a farming family, there was no reason for Isolda to know how to read or write. Her only job was to work in the fields and help care for her family. Peasant children didn't go to school, but boys from wealthy families may have.

Peasant girls in the Middle Ages learned to cook, clean, and weave, while peasant boys learned how to farm and care for animals. They may have learned a skill such as shoemaking, pottery, or blacksmithing. Some peasant children were allowed to work in the lord's home, either in the kitchen or in the **stable**.

Children learned the skills they needed to take care of their own family one day.

17

RELIGION AND FEASTS

Religion was a big part of life in the Middle Ages. Isolda's family went to church on Sundays and on **saints'** days, or holidays that honored important people in religious history. Peasants couldn't read, so they listened as **priests** read from special books during a church mass. That's how they learned about their religion.

RELIGIOUS ART

Much of the art that was created during the Middle Ages shows religious stories and was kept in churches, which were built to honor God.

Feast days gave Isolda a chance to play with her friends, since they didn't have to work.

Peasants worked hard, but they had fun, too. They had big feasts to celebrate saints' days and events such as when crops were harvested, or gathered. On these days, peasants went to church, ate special food, danced, and sang. It was a nice break from their normal life of hard work.

THE BLACK DEATH

If you lived during the Middle Ages, you might have thought it was very stinky. That's because people didn't take baths or wash their clothes very often! In fact, the only people who did this were the rich. Even then, it didn't occur very often.

Piles of garbage lined the streets in Isolda's village. This **attracted** rats that had bugs called fleas living on them. The fleas carried **diseases** that made people sick. One of the worst diseases was the plague, also known as the Black Death. It killed millions of people across Europe. Children and babies who got sick usually died.

SPOTS OF SICKNESS

People who got the plague developed large, purplish-black spots on their neck, arms, and other areas of the body.

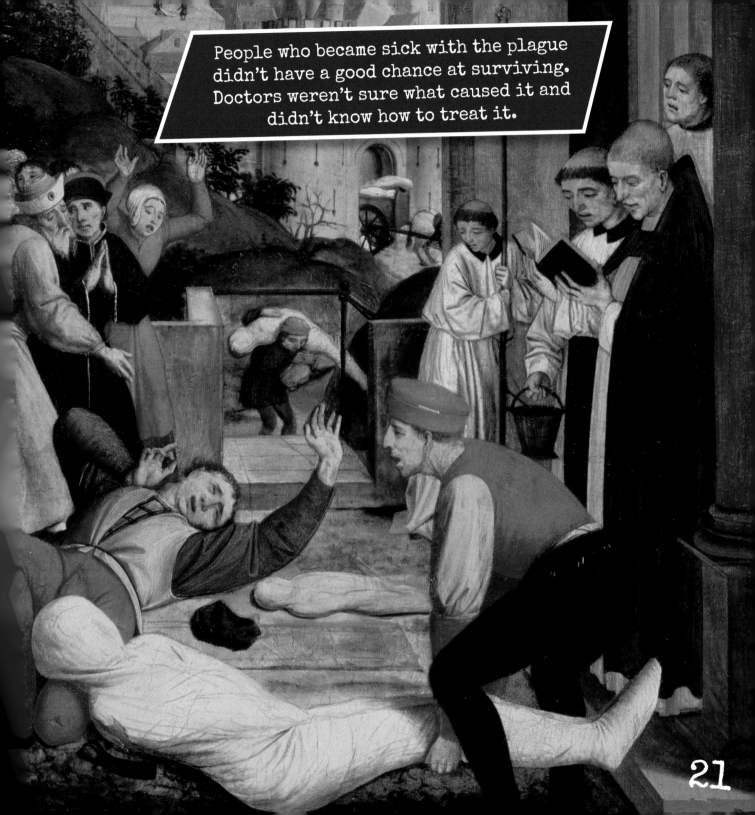

People who became sick with the plague didn't have a good chance at surviving. Doctors weren't sure what caused it and didn't know how to treat it.

21

MAKING DO

Life in the Middle Ages was hard. Peasant children were born into a life of work. They faced terrible diseases and unclean conditions. Many children died when they were very young. Even children from rich families died young, though their chances of living longer were better.

Despite their hardships, children in the Middle Ages grew up to become adults with their own family. These people celebrated their religion, had fun on feast days, and worked hard. In the 1,000 years this time period lasted, people of the Middle Ages did the best with what they had.

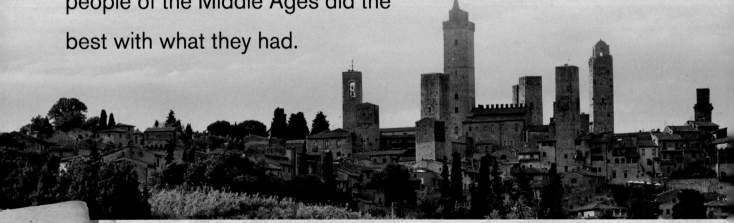

GLOSSARY

attract: To draw in.

culture: The beliefs and ways of life of a group of people.

disease: Sickness.

elaborate: Involving many carefully arranged parts, details, or decorations.

era: A long period of history.

hearth: A fireplace.

institution: An organization that is created for a certain purpose, such as a church.

jewelry: Pieces of metal, plastic, or other matter worn as decoration.

priest: A person who performs religious ceremonies.

religion: A belief in and way of honoring a god or gods.

saint: An important person in religious history.

stable: A barn for animals.

INDEX

WEBSITES

Due to the changing nature of Internet links, PowerKids Press has developed an online list of websites related to the subject of this book. This site is updated regularly. Please use this link to access the list: www.powerkidslinks.com/hkl/mddl